To Nathan,

Believe in Yourself!

You Can do Anything!

Jan Newall

Galaxy Pizza

And Other School Poems That Are Out of This World!

and Meteor Pie

Poems by
Darren Sardelli

Illustrations by
Pam Catapano

Laugh-A-Lot Books
New York

Publisher's Cataloging-in-Publication (provided by Quality Books, Inc.)

Sardelli, Darren.
    Galaxy pizza and meteor pie: and other school poems
  that are out of this world! / by Darren Sardelli;
  illustrated by Pam Catapano.
      p. cm.
    Summary: A collection of funny rhyming poems for elementary and middle school students. School life is the focus,
  including a teacher who mixes up her words, one who gives detention to water fountains, lunch ladies who serve
  Milky Way shakes and fresh corn on the comet, and a principal who lets kids take over the school on Opposite Day.
    LCCN 2009902459
    ISBN-13: 978-0-615-28469-9
    ISBN-10: 0-615-28469-8

    1. Children's poetry, American. 2. Humorous poetry, American. [1. Humorous poetry. 2. American poetry.] I. Catapano, Pam, ill. II. Title.

    PS3619.A725G35 2009   811'.6
              QBI09-600062

Editor: Angela Wiechmann
Production Manager and Design: Paul Woods
Illustrations: Pam Catapano

Published by Laugh-A-Lot Books, 25 West Broadway, Suite 310, Long Beach, New York 11561

www.laughalotbooks.com   www.laughalotpoetry.com

19 18 17   10 9 8 7 6 5 4

Printed in China

Credits

"My Doggy Ate My Essay", "Parent-Teacher Conference", and "A Work of Art" copyright © 2006, previously published in *My Teacher's in Detention* (Meadowbrook Press), "Science Test" copyright © 2008, previously published in *Buses To Books* (ABDO Publishing), "A Snowman with a Carrot Nose" copyright © 2006, previously published in *The 2009 Dutch Farmer's Almanac* (Kluis Publishing), "Recess! Oh, Recess!" was inspired by Jack Prelutsky's poem "Homework! Oh, Homework!" and "Science Test" was inspired by Shel Silverstein's poem "Sick".

Acknowledgments

Thank you! Thank you! Thank you!

My parents, Rosemary and Joseph, my brothers, Ryan, Kevin, Nolan, and Jonathan, my friends and family– Thank you for believing in me. You have all inspired me in many ways.

Bruce Lansky—Thank you for giving me the opportunity to work on projects for your company.

Angie Wiechmann and Paul Woods—Thank you for helping me put this book together. I appreciate all of your hard work on this project.

Monte Schulz—Thank you for showing me how a poem should be written. Many doors have opened since our first conversation.

L.I.C.W.I. (Long Island Children's Writers and Illustrators)—Thank you for your love and support. You're all amazing people as well as incredible artists.

Theodor and Shel—Thank you for helping me find my purpose in life. You guys rock!

Ida, Peggy, Lou, and Paul—Thank you for the world! It is an honor being your grandson.

All of the people who enjoy my poetry—Thank you for your letters, emails, and comments. I appreciate all of your support.

A Note from the Illustrator

This collection of art is dedicated to my two handsome sons, Alix and Zack. It was through their eyes that I was fortunate enough to see the beauty in my surroundings. As I grew up on Long Island, my life had been filled with wonderful people and memories. This art is a reflection of them all. My love for children has inspired me to create whimsy with color and character. To all the children out there, this is for you.

—Pam Catapano

Contents

Dedication
This book is dedicated to all of the
people who don't like poetry.
(I used to be one of those people.)

Galaxy Pizza and Meteor Pie

Those wonderful ladies have done it again.
Their meals are like magic. Their food is a ten.
They lit up the lunchroom and brightened our day
by serving hot lunch on a Tentacle Tray.

Their menu consisted of Jupiter Steaks
with Astronaut Apples and Milky Way Shakes.
Their Mercury Muffins were yummy and sweet.
Their Corn on the Comet was everyone's treat.

My friends were impressed with the Cheese from the Moon.
We slurped Saturn Soup from an Orbiting Spoon.
The ladies surprised us with Clusters on Rye,
a Galaxy Pizza, and Meteor Pie.

Their Nebula Nachos had Asteroid Chips.
Their Candy Cane Craters produced an Eclipse.
The lunch in our lunchroom is rated five Stars.
I'm glad that these lunch ladies came here from Mars!

Here Come the Girls

Margaret Mullen kicked a ball,
which hit me on the chin.
Sara Soda smacked a puck,
which nicked me on my shin.
Polly Pepper knocked me down
while running 'round the track.
Nora Noodles tossed the disc
that landed on my snack.
Bonnie Brownie swung her cleats
and bopped me on the head.
Laura Lemon splashed my pants,
which made my face turn red.
Gabby Giggles threw her stick,
which ripped my favorite shorts.
I always have a great time
when I watch the girls play sports.

The Silliest Teacher in School

Our teacher gave detention
to the fountains in the hall.
She handed extra homework
to the artwork on the wall.

We saw her point a finger
at a banner and a sign.
She said their bad behavior
was completely out of line.

The principal approached her
and said, "What is all this fuss?
I heard you tried to punish
all the tires on a bus.

"You've made the teachers angry
by disrupting all their classes,
so if you want to keep this job,
you have to wear your glasses!"

A Call from Principal Schaefer

Principal Schaefer took my gum
and brought me to the office.
As we were walking down the hall,
I felt a little nauseous.
She called my mom at work and said,
"Your daughter broke a rule.
Although she is a teacher here,
she can't chew gum in school."

My Doggy Ate My Essay

My doggy ate my essay.
He picked up all my mail.
He cleaned my dirty closet
and dusted with his tail.

He straightened out my posters
and swept my wooden floor.
My parents almost fainted
when he fixed my bedroom door.

I did not try to stop him.
He made my windows shine.
My room looked like a palace,
and my dresser smelled like pine.

He fluffed up every pillow.
He folded all my clothes.
He even cleaned my fish tank
with a toothbrush and a hose.

I thought it was amazing
to see him use a broom.
I'm glad he ate my essay
on "How to Clean My Room."

Our Teacher Has Amnesia

Miss Bell could not remember
all the chapters we had read.
She must have got amnesia
when that pot fell on her head.
Although it was untruthful
and a little bit unkind,
we said we'd finished reading
all the books she had assigned.

We told her math and science
were the subjects to ignore.
We made a claim that homework
was a dreadful, boring chore.
We chatted on our cell phones
and chewed gum throughout the day.
We let her think the classroom
was a place to run and play.

The day was almost over
when Miss Bell picked up the pot.
The pot made her remember
all the things she had forgot.
She placed it on a floating shelf,
then walked around the room.
I saw the fury in her eyes
and felt a sense of doom.

When Miss Bell blew her whistle,
we were all consumed with fear.
She gave the class detention
the remainder of the year.
She made a threat to give us
extra homework every night.
She also said, "At recess,
we will stay inside and write!"

The fish began to tremble
as she raised her angry voice.
She shook her head and told us
we had made an awful choice.
The pot fell off the shelf again
and bonked her on the head,
and once again, Miss Bell forgot
the things that she had said.

BONK

A Snowman with
a Carrot Nose

A snowman with a carrot nose
is not considered wise.
My teacher said that carrots
are essential for your *eyes*.

Squash That Bug!

We need to stop the Flu Bug!
She's resting by a brook.
Before she makes your tummy ache,
Please quickly close this book!

The Ghost of Mrs. Rose

In an old, abandoned lunchroom
in a dark, deserted school,
with a kitchen full of cobwebs,
where the air is damp and cool,
lives a cold and creepy lady
with spaghetti on her clothes.
She's the one who served the lunches.
She's the ghost of Mrs. Rose.

Now, I never thought a lady
could be vicious, mean, or cruel,
till I heard the awful stories
of the things she did in school.
She'd make students eat their veggies
and the meatloaf on their plate
and would gladly serve them seconds
when they finished what they ate.

She made sure that every student
washed their hands before a meal
and suggested fish and liver
would improve the way they feel.
She would keep them off the playground
if they didn't clean their mess
and would often give them lectures
on the proper way to dress.

There were days she'd make them listen
to the stories in the news,
and she'd check for sloppy laces
on their sneakers and their shoes.
She was known for blowing whistles
when a student tried to nap
and insisted messy eaters
kept a napkin on their lap.

There are many spooky stories
'bout the things she used to do.
She reminded every student
that they shouldn't talk and chew.
If a lady in your lunchroom
is a nuisance or a pest,
please be on your best behavior
'cause she just might be possessed!

People Like to Push Me

People like to push me,
but I never say a word.
You may find this ridiculous
and even quite absurd.

People like to sit on me.
They do this all the time.
They even put their feet on me
and cover me with grime.

They've twisted me! They've tangled me!
They've tied me in a knot!
They leave me in the pouring rain!
They grab me when it's hot!

People like to push me,
but I never say a thing.
It's nice to see them having fun—
it's great to be a swing.

Recess! Oh, Recess!

Recess! Oh, Recess!
We love you! You rule!
You keep us away
from the teachers in school.
Your swings are refreshing.
Your slides are the best.
You give us a break
from a really hard test.

Recess! Oh, Recess!
We want you to know,
you're sweeter than syrup,
you're special like snow.
You don't assign homework.
You make the day fun.
You let us play kickball
and run in the sun.

Recess! Oh, Recess!
You're first on our list.
We'd be in despair
if you didn't exist.
We're happy we have you.
You're awesome and cool.
Recess! Oh, Recess!
We love you! You rule!

Parent-Teacher Conference

At the parent-teacher conference,
my father made a scene.
He scared my fifth-grade teacher
with his mask from Halloween.

She showed him all my science grades
and said she was concerned,
but he just stuck his tongue out
when my teacher's back was turned.

He drew a monster on the board
and claimed it was her twin.
He even shook her soda,
which exploded on her chin.

My angry teacher crossed her arms
and said, "This meeting's done!
I now see where he gets it from—
you act just like your son!"

Opposite Day

The principal shouted,
"It's Opposite Day!
Pick up your assignments
and put them away.
I'm ordering pizza.
I'm handing out gum.
I'm playing my trumpet
and banging my drum.
It's time to get rowdy.
It's time to be pests.
There will be no homework,
no quizzes or tests.
Let's jump on the tables.
Let's run in the halls.
Let's grab every marker
and draw on the walls.
It's your day to party.
It's your day to shine.
It's your day to cut
to the front of the line.
So listen to music
and swing from the plants.
Replace every poster
with polka dot pants.
Let's clog up the toilets
with gym shorts and clay.
You get to be bad
'cause it's Opposite Day.
You're free to watch movies
and climb up the swings.
You won't get in trouble
for doing these things.
And last but not least,
if you think this is cool,
you'll always be known
as a big *April fool!*"

Science Test

I think I failed my science test.
My stomach's tied in knots.
My ears are clogged, my nose is stuffed,
I'm seeing purple spots.
I cannot feel my toes or feet.
My arms are very weak.
My back is in tremendous pain.
It's difficult to speak.
I should have been excused today,
but Mom said I looked fine.
I think my fever should have been
a giant warning sign!
I cannot breathe! I'm turning blue!
There's something on my chest—
What's that you say?
I got an *A?*
I knew I passed this test!

The Awful Truth

When Dribs auditioned for the play,
he messed up all his lines.
The script was right in front of him.
His teacher held up signs.
He stood there like a statue,
staring blankly at the scene,
embarrassed by the awful truth:
He had to kiss a queen.

NOUN = A person, place or thing

VERB = An action word

A,E,I,O,U

Fiction - Does not represent actuality.

NON Fiction - Presented as fact.

Two great ways of expressing ones ideas.

READ A BOOK

POETRY

ADJECTIVE = modifies a noun or a pronoun.

WRITE A BOOK

Erasing the Board

I thought my teacher would be proud
when I erased the board.

I thought she'd say, "Terrific Job!"
and give me a reward.

I thought the students in my class
would smile, clap, and cheer.

I never thought the chalkboard
would completely disappear.

A Work of Art

I followed her directions.
I did what she had said.
I painted with my paintbrush
and used the color red.

I drew with magic markers
and made a nice design.
I took my wooden chisel
and carved a perfect line.

Before the class was over,
I showed her what I did.
When I saw her reaction,
I almost ran and hid.

I followed her directions!
I thought I'd get a star!
Instead I got detention
for my artwork on her car.

24

A Party on Halloween Night

My school had a party on Halloween night.
The big jack-o'-lanterns were orange and bright.
The witches were flying around on their brooms.
The mummies were dancing inside of their tombs.
The werewolves were howling and climbing the walls.
The ghosts kept appearing in doorways and halls.
A goblin was stuck in a seven-foot web,
and Bigfoot was chasing a zombie named Zeb.

I ran into monsters who live under beds;
a few of these monsters have seventeen heads.
A wizard was dancing with Frankenstein's mother.
A bat and a phantom were kissing each other.
I noticed a bloodstain on Dracula's shirt.
The ogres were feasting on Eyeball Dessert.
I wasn't afraid of these Halloween creatures,
but ran out the door when I saw all my teachers.

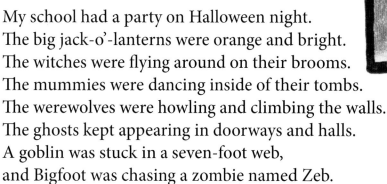

A Far-Out Family

My father is an astronaut.
My mom observes the stars.
My sister wrote eleven books
on Mercury and Mars.

My uncle owns a telescope;
he likes to watch the moon.
My grandma claims a UFO
will be here very soon.

My brother is a scientist
who photographs the sun.
My cousin thinks astronomy
is wonderful and fun.

They all came to my science fair
and talked to Miss McGrace,
who said the only thing I do
is take up *time* and *space*.

I Blow a Tissue with My Nose

I blow a tissue with my nose
and pencil with a write.
I always chair down in a sit
and bed to go at night.

My favorite cake is chocolate food
with side cream on the whip.
When I board off a diving jump,
I double do a flip.

I brush a toothbrush with my teeth
and wash my soap with face.
I like to shower in the sing
and crayon with a trace.

It's nice to sky the sunny watch
and bay beside the lay.
I wonder laugh my students why
when what they hear I say.

Fun Facts About the Author

Favorite comic strips:	*Peanuts, Garfield, Dennis the Menace*
Favorite sports:	Ice hockey, baseball, tennis, X Games
Favorite foods:	Spaghetti and meatballs, chicken noodle soup, chocolate chip pancakes
Favorite fruits and vegetables:	Strawberries, apples, carrots, corn
Favorite poets:	Shel Silverstein, Dr. Seuss, Judith Viorst, Mary Ann Hoberman, the poets at Meadowbrook Press
Favorite animals:	Dogs, parrots, kangaroos
Favorite bubblegum flavors:	Grape and cherry
Favorite color:	Green
Favorite artists:	Thomas Kinkade, Pam Catapano
Favorite activities in school:	Gym, recess, and lunch
Favorite parts of my job:	Using my imagination, visiting schools, making people laugh
Favorite website:	www.laughalotpoetry.com

If I Can Do It, You Can Do It, Too!

Before the age of twenty, I had no idea I wanted to be a writer. In fact, if someone told me I was going to be a poet twelve years ago, I would have laughed and said they were crazy. I used to think poetry was boring and wanted nothing to do with it. After an inspirational dream in college, I decided to write a poem for fun. Truthfully, I didn't think it would amount to anything, but I was curious to see what I was capable of. My first poem wasn't very good, but I had fun writing it. I enjoyed using my imagination, coming up with different scenarios, and thinking of words that rhyme. From that day on, I began to write down my ideas. I started working on projects for different publishing companies in 2004 and now my poems are featured in fifteen children's books (eight in the U.S. and seven in the U.K). I've also visited hundreds of schools and libraries all over the country.

It took me a long time to write this book, but I finally did it! I would have never discovered my talent for writing poetry if I hadn't given it a shot. There are so many people in this world who are capable of doing great things, but they're too afraid to try. I challenge each and every one of you to try new things. Be brave, face your fears, and show the world what you're made of. As long as you believe in yourself, you can achieve anything!

Work hard and good things will happen!